LANA VAWSER

A TIME TO *Selah*

All emphasis within Scripture quotations is the author's own.

DESTINY IMAGE® PUBLISHERS, INC.

PO Box 310, Shippensburg, PA 17257-0310

"Promoting Inspired Lives"

This book and all other Destiny Image and Destiny Image Fiction books are available at Christian bookstores and distributors worldwide.

For more information on foreign distributors, call 717-532-3040.

Or reach us on the Internet: www.destinyimage.com

ISBN 13 TP: 978-0-7684-5674-5

ISBN 13 EBook: 978-0-7684-5664-6

For Worldwide Distribution, Printed in the U.S.A.

1 2 3 4 5 6 / 23 22 21 20

Contents

Chapter 1

A Garden Confrontation

As I sit here in my office, the whole world has been placed on pause. Here I sit as the news loudly reports on the Coronavirus and how it has spread, the damage it has caused, and the scrambling to bring protection to people of the world from this virus.

Nations are on lockdown. State borders are closed. People have died. People are sick. People are fearful. People are losing and have lost their jobs. The future seems uncertain. The questions resound loudly in hearts and out of people's mouths, "When will this end?" "Will life ever go back to normal?" "What will the ramifications of this be in the earth?"

I remember sitting with the Lord when this Coronavirus began to spread into the nations. I sat in my favorite corner of the lounge looking out at my beautiful garden with a hot coffee in hand and seeking the Lord's heart for what He was saying amid the "noise" bombarding the airwaves. That's when I heard His whisper, "Lana, I am inviting My people back to the Garden with Me. It's a SELAH moment."

Immediately I knew what the Lord was inviting us into. The Garden speaks to me of intimacy. It speaks to me of communing with Him and walking with Him in the cool of the day (Genesis 3:8). I thought of the word *"selah"* and its meaning—the invitation to *pause* and *reflect.*

I continued to seek His heart and He whispered again, "There is fire in the Garden. I am inviting My people into the Garden to be *aligned, refined, and purified.*"

I received those words for my own life and heard my heart crying out to Him, "Lord, I embrace Your fire! Holy Spirit, do whatever You have to do in me to align me, refine me, and purify me in greater ways." The sense then surrounded me so strongly that this was a very significant moment of preparation—and what struck me so strongly was what the Lord spoke next:

"Lana, the encounters and lessons learned in this moment with Me for My people are going to be things that they carry into this new era."

We are here in a "forced" lockdown around the earth, but I feel the hand of the Lord. What I am writing here is not just for this moment on earth where we are now, historically, seeing the coronavirus spread—I believe the Lord is bringing the Church into a depth in Him that we have never experienced.

Right now we are being led into a place of surrender that's deeper than we have ever faced. Churches are closed. Services are cancelled. Conferences are cancelled.

Life as normal is no longer life as normal.

So right now, friend, I believe the Holy Spirit is inviting us into a place in the Garden with Him to lay ourselves down. There is a call right now upon the Church as a whole and upon us as individuals to lay ourselves down.

We are in a moment of fresh surrender. I hear Romans 12:1-2 (NKJV) resounding loudly:

> *I beseech you therefore, brethren, by the mercies of God, that you present your bodies a living sacrifice, holy, acceptable to God, which is your reasonable service. And do not be conformed to this world, but be transformed by the renewing of your mind, that you may prove what is that good and acceptable and perfect will of God.*

This *selah* invitation is to pause and reflect right now. To rewrite in other way: God is inviting you and me into the place of deep surrender where we place everything on the altar and allow His fire to fall and consume what needs to be consumed and to strengthen and refine what remains.

I find it interesting that the word "corona" means crown. The Lord is dealing with pride, and the King of Glory is going to take His place. For the past few weeks I have been hearing the Matt Redman song, "We Fall Down." I believe this is a song for the hour that describes the invitation being placed before us:

We fall down
We lay our crowns
At the feet of Jesus
The greatness of
Mercy and love
At the feet of Jesus.

And we cry holy, holy, holy
And we cry holy, holy, holy
And we cry holy, holy, holy
Is the Lamb.

We fall down
We lay our crowns
At the feet of Jesus
The greatness of
Mercy and love
At the feet of Jesus.

And we cry holy, holy, holy
And we cry holy, holy, holy
And we cry holy, holy, holy
Is the Lamb.

We fall down
We lay our crowns
At the feet of Jesus
The greatness of
Mercy and love
At the feet of Jesus.

(Written by Phil Wickham, Matt Redman, Brian Johnson (Bethel), Brandon Lake, 2020)

There is a call right now to lay down our crowns before the feet of Jesus. King Jesus is going to be exalted!

I feel the love of God so strongly for His people right now. He is calling us higher. He is calling us into our place of authority and positioning for this new era. This is the love of God that is giving us room to respond to Him and position ourselves for what is to come.

For many years now the Lord has been speaking to me these words, "Ready or not, here I come"—and friend, I feel those words stronger than ever right now. The invitation we are faced with right now is an invitation to go deeper into His heart. It is an invitation to prepare ourselves.

The Bible says in Revelation 19:7 (NIV): *"Let us rejoice and be glad and give him glory! For the wedding of the Lamb has come, and his bride has made herself ready."* There is a depth of preparation that the Lord is inviting us into right now and it comes in the position of surrender.

This is a decisive moment. This is a moment when the Lord is calling us to align. This is one of the moments when the Lord is beckoning us to align with what He is doing and what He is saying. This is the time in the Garden with Him when we are called to a place of decision. We are called to the place of confronting comforts.

We are in a place where we are called to face areas of control. This is the beautiful, glorious place where fears are confronted. This is the beautiful, glorious place where anxiety is confronted. This is the place where agendas are confronted.

This is the place of confrontation in the Garden and it's a beautiful place. Why? Because Jesus is there. The Healer is there. The Deliverer is there. The Refiner is there. The Word is there. The Comforter is there.

This is the place where we lay ourselves down and truly invite the Holy Spirit to come and examine our hearts in the light of His presence (Psalm 139:23-24) and come into alignment with His ways. What do I mean by this? When all of our "normal life" is being shaken up and turned upside down, where do we turn? Where do we look? Where do we lean? Where do we align? We look to Jesus.

Oh the resounding invitation I hear for the Church to throw herself completely into the arms of God in surrender and be brought back deeply to the place of our First Love for Him. Friend, the encounters upon you in this moment right now and in this new era as we continue to journey with Him are unprecedented. The revelation and unveiling of Jesus right now that is awaiting you and I in this Garden place is astonishing.

The Holy Spirit has been so heavy upon me in the past few days and He has been repeating many phrases. One of those phrases is: "Lana, this is the point where everything changes. Nothing remains the same from this point on." I believe that this a point where things have changed and will continue to change. This is the place where we as the Church need to make a decision on where we stand and where we sit.

This is a call to be on the right side of the fence. This is the time to be totally surrendered to Him. This is the time to be completely consumed by His fire and prepared by His Spirit and refined by His Word. This is the place where you will experience His presence like never before. This is where God wants to meet you deeply, in life-changing ways. This is the place where God is going to encounter you so deeply, where everything will change.

I heard the Lord say, "Not only does everything change from this point on, this is the point where My *people* change."

This is the time when the body of Christ is being invited back into the Garden—to come back to our First Love for Him. Where fear has occupied your heart, where doubt has occupied your heart, where lies have occupied your heart, where other loves have occupied your heart, where sin has entangled, where things have held you back from being all you can be in Christ and running with Him in the empowerment of the Spirit in ways you never dreamed—this is the time when it happens. This is the place where you become more of the *you* He created you to be as you surrender afresh again.

I see wave upon wave upon wave of His love crashing over you in the Garden. I see tears of repentance that fall to the ground and the embrace of His loving, strong arms, surrounding you as your place of safety and your refuge (Psalm 91).

The revelations and lessons learned right now are tools for this journey, they are tools to navigate the new territory ahead. So when this coronavirus passes, yes ***when***, because it will, the revelation and the lessons learned in this moment are going to be *tools* for you to *build* with Him in this new era. That's why He is inviting us to *pause*. This isn't just about the moment on earth of battling a virus that the enemy is having a field day with—this is about a moment of *birthing* in the body of Christ for those who will *hear* the sound of the invitation of the Lord right now to *come away, to pause and reflect*.

I believe this *selah* invitation is a revelation and a key for this new era. It is the place the Lord wants us to *remember* and *live from*. Let me explain. We are in a season of unprecedented acceleration. We are seeing that in the negative, in the natural, how fast this virus is spreading, *but*, we look not to the earth and the natural realm, we look to Jesus, we look to what He is doing.

There is significant acceleration taking place on earth right now and the Lord is moving rapidly. But *in* the acceleration, there is a temptation to get busy and to get caught up in doing things for God and even having our hands to building the Kingdom. There is nothing wrong with building; God wants us to build. But if building takes the place of focus of intimacy with Him or keeps us so busy we feel like we are constantly going from one thing to the next, then we need to slow down. This *selah* invitation from the Lord is a wake-up call and reminder to us that we live *from* the Garden, and we have to be people who are first and foremost ministering to Him.

I want you to absorb this, our focus must be on ministering first and foremost to Him. This is a place of deep healing. This is a place of deep deliverance. This is a place of deep freedom for those who will hear and embrace the shaking and steward well this moment with Him. This isn't a time to be in fear. This is a time to draw close and ask Him what He is doing, what He is saying. Oh the expectancy in my spirit for this moment. This is where we are birthed if we embrace what He is doing.

I was making my coffee the other morning and the voice of the Lord thundered over me so loudly it shook me. He spoke these words, "Lana, I am forging and forming the true *Ecclesia*." The *Ecclesia* is the universal Church—the body of Christ on earth.

Immediately the understanding came to me. In this shifting and in this shaking there is a *sifting* taking place. God is sifting. He is looking for those who are "all in." He is looking for those who are moving with Him and their hearts are fully surrendered to Him. This is the place where God is looking for those who are all about Him and His ways and His agenda. He is desperately longing and looking for those who want His heart.

When He spoke these words, He undid me to the core, "Lana, I am looking for those who want MY HEART."

When He spoke those words, I was undone by the invitation. This is a time to receive the heart of God. This is a time to hear what God is saying. This is a time to receive His heart of love for yourself and for others. This is a time to receive His perspective and wisdom. This is a time to really see what is on the heart of God. Think about that for a moment. Not an invitation to hear what your next door neighbor is saying—this is an invitation to hear deeper than you ever have what is on the King of king's heart. This is an invitation right now to see what the King of kings is building and dreaming about.

It is right now an invitation to partner with His blueprints and strategies for the greatest move of the Spirit of God upon the earth. Is it urgent? Absolutely! Why? Because the King of Glory is coming! (Psalm 24:7-9) He's coming, ready or not. He wants you ready! He wants me ready! He wants us to be in a place where our lamps are full of oil (Matthew 25).

There is a purification taking place of heart motives; the question being asked, "What do you want more?" It's not a question of condemnation, it's a question that calls us higher. It's a question that aligns.

In the Garden place as His Spirit falls heavily upon you, those desires are coming to the surface; and as the Holy Spirit is embraced to do His work, the fire of His presence is consuming any other desire and He is imparting His fire, the fire of His love and presence in weight we have never before experienced—and the *burning ones are being birthed.*

Who are the burning ones? Those who give their whole lives. Those whose hearts are living and burning in adoration for Jesus first and foremost. This is a threshing floor, friend. This is a glorious threshing floor in preparation for what's ahead.

Pruning for Promotion

As I looked out my window into the garden the other day I saw where my beautiful roses were...and all of a sudden I noticed they weren't there anymore. They were gone. I gasped aloud as I noticed they had been pruned. The gardener had come and pruned my roses and I was so shocked. I said to myself, "I can't believe he pruned back my roses."

Immediately the Holy Spirit spoke to me: "Lana, many have been surprised by this moment and many have been surprised by the *pruning* that is taking place right now, but the *pruning must* take place for the *promotion* that is ahead. Those who embrace the *pruning* will be *prepared* for the *promotion*."

Wow did that ever ring deeply in my spirit.

The Gardner has come. He has arrived and He has come suddenly and unexpectedly. What the enemy meant for harm (Genesis 50:20), God is using for good. The hand of the Lord is moving here and the Gardener has suddenly showed up to prune for the *promotion* that's coming. There is a great promotion coming upon the faithful and upon those who embrace this move of His Spirit.

The Lord continued to speak, "I am removing the weeds. I am weeding out the weeds."

The Lord is removing the weeds in the Garden. He is removing the weeds in the lives of His people individually, and He is removing the weeds in the Church. He is removing the impurity, He is removing control, He is removing all things that hinder and entangle all that He is doing and about to do. He is inviting us to remove the weeds with Him (Song of Songs 2:15).

This is the Isaiah 60 time. It is not just for this moment as we see the coronavirus pandemic. There will be other trials, other hardships, and others battles that will come; and as the darkness covers the earth, it's the time for the Church to arise and shine. But in order for the Church to arise and shine, she must be one who lives in the place of First Love. Her wholehearted devotion first and foremost is to Him and His ways.

This shift right now is inviting you and me back to school with the Holy Spirit. This is the time to invite Him to come and teach us afresh. From this point on, how things were done won't remain. There is an upgrade. There is a new wineskin. There's new wine. There is a greater invitation to understand and follow His ways (Isaiah 55:11).

This is a time to step into deeper surrender and walk deeper in the wisdom of God (Proverbs 4:6-7). This is the place where we recognize more than ever that God is doing a new thing (Isaiah 43:19), and we are being called to position, get ready, to catch the wave. Malachi 3:2-4 (NKJV) tells us:

> *But who can endure the day of His coming? And who can stand when He appears? For He is like a refiner's fire and like launderers' soap. He will sit as a refiner and a purifier of silver; He will purify the sons of Levi, and purge them as gold and silver, that they may offer to the Lord an offering in righteousness. Then the offering of Judah and Jerusalem will be pleasant to the Lord, as in the days of old, as in former years.*

Our lives are our offering, let our offering to the Lord be pure, be holy.

I heard His whisper this week, "Lana, listen closely, can you hear the sound of reformation?"

"YES, LORD, I hear the sound of reformation."

It's here, friend. This is the sound of reformation. The call from the Lord is going out to one and all in the body of Christ. STOP. LIE DOWN AND LISTEN!

The answer to the call is found in the Garden, in surrender. There's fire in the Garden. The reformation of the Church is upon us. I'm embracing what He is doing, friend.

This is where you arise and shine and move into your greatest days with the Lord on earth and the place of seeing His power demonstrated in and through your life in unprecedented ways. *This is* actually the place of a *major* breakthrough and shifting of alignment in Him.

As Brian Johnson says, "Consider it a gift when God becomes your only option."

Look at this *selah* moment as a gift. It's a gift because stewarded properly; it is giving you tools to navigate the new era. But the greatest gift is this—you move deeper into the revelation and manifestation that *He* is your greatest reward.

In the pruning, you meet the Gardner like you never have before.

I want to close this chapter with the lyrics from Cody Carnes' new song "Nothing Else." This song encapsulates so much of the heart of God and the alignment taking place. The new sound arising. We are coming back to and deeper into Psalm 84:2:

> *My soul longs, yes, faints for the courts of the Lord; my heart and flesh sing for joy to the living God* (ESV).
>
> *Deep within me are these lovesick longings, desires and daydreams of living in union with you. When I'm near you my heart and my soul will sing and worship with my joyful songs of you, my true source and spring of life!* (TPT)

Can I encourage you to purchase this song, listen to it online, meditate on the lyrics here and allow the Holy Spirit to draw you deeper into the Garden with Him.

I'm caught up in Your presence
I just want to sit here at Your feet
I'm caught up in this holy moment
I never want to leave.

Oh, I'm not here for blessings

Jesus, You don't owe me anything
More than anything that You can do
I just want You.

I'm sorry when I've just gone through
the motions
I'm sorry when I just sang another song
Take me back to where we started
I open up my heart to You.

I'm sorry when I've come with my agenda
I'm sorry when I forgot that
You're enough
Take me back to where we started
I open up my heart to You.

I just want You
Nothing else, nothing else
Nothing else will do

I just want You
Nothing else, nothing else
Nothing else will do
I just want You
Nothing else, nothing else
Nothing else will do
I just want You
Nothing else, nothing else, Jesus
Nothing else will do
I just want You
Nothing else, nothing else
Nothing else will do
I just want You
Nothing else, nothing else, Jesus
Nothing else will do.

I'm coming back to where we started
I'm coming back to where we started
When I first felt Your love

You're all that matters, Jesus
You're all that matters
I'm coming back to what really matters
Just Your heart
I just want to bless Your heart, Jesus.

I'm caught up in Your presence
I just want to sit here at Your feet
I'm caught up in this holy moment
I never want to leave.

And oh, I'm not here for blessings
Jesus, You don't owe me anything
More than anything that You can do
Oh, I just want You.

Songwriters: Cody Carnes,
Hank Bentley, Jessie Early

Chapter 2

"I Am Raising Up a People Possessed with My Divine Strategy"

Over the past few weeks, the Lord has highlighted three biblical characters to me:

1. Elijah
2. Noah
3. Joseph

As I sat with the Lord and recognized that all three of these biblical characters the Lord has had me release prophetic words from different areas of their lives over the last few years. Then something hit me recently as I saw a common theme in all three of their lives—*divine strategy!*

Let's look at this revelation through Scripture:

1. Elijah

> *Then Elijah said to Ahab, "Go up, eat and drink; for there is the sound of abundance of*

> *rain." So Ahab went up to eat and drink. And Elijah went up to the top of Carmel; then he bowed down on the ground, and put his face between his knees, and said to his servant, "Go up now, look toward the sea." So he went up and looked, and said, "There is nothing." And seven times he said, "Go again." Then it came to pass the seventh time, that he said, "There is a cloud, as small as a man's hand, rising out of the sea!" So he said, "Go up, say to Ahab, 'Prepare your chariot, and go down before the rain stops you.'" Now it happened in the meantime that the sky became black with clouds and wind, and there was a heavy rain. So Ahab rode away and went to Jezreel* (1 Kings 18:41-45 NKJV).

2. Noah

> *The Lord saw that the wickedness of man was great in the earth, and that every intention of the thoughts of his heart was only evil continually. And the Lord regretted that he had made man on the earth, and it grieved him to his heart. So the Lord said, "I will blot out man*

whom I have created from the face of the land, man and animals and creeping things and birds of the heavens, for I am sorry that I have made them." But Noah found favor in the eyes of the Lord.

Noah and the Flood

These are the generations of Noah. Noah was a righteous man, blameless in his generation. Noah walked with God. And Noah had three sons, Shem, Ham, and Japheth.

Now the earth was corrupt in God's sight, and the earth was filled with violence. And God saw the earth, and behold, it was corrupt, for all flesh had corrupted their way on the earth. And God said to Noah, "I have determined to make an end of all flesh, for the earth is filled with violence through them. Behold, I will destroy them with the earth. Make yourself an ark of gopher wood. Make rooms in the ark, and cover it inside and out with pitch. This is how you are to make it: the length of the ark 300 cubits, its breadth 50 cubits, and its height 30 cubits. Make a roof for the ark, and finish it to a cubit above, and set the door of the ark in its side. Make it with lower, second, and third decks.

For behold, I will bring a flood of waters upon the earth to destroy all flesh in which is the breath of life under heaven. Everything that is on the earth shall die. But I will establish my covenant with you, and you shall come into the ark, you, your sons, your wife, and your sons' wives with you. And of every living thing of all flesh, you shall bring two of every sort into the ark to keep them alive with you. They shall be male and female. Of the birds according to their kinds, and of the animals according to their kinds, of every creeping thing of the ground, according to its kind, two of every sort shall come in to you to keep them alive. Also take with you every sort of food that is eaten, and store it up. It shall serve as food for you and for them." Noah did this; he did all that God commanded him (Genesis 6:5-21 ESV).

Then the Lord said to Noah, "Go into the ark, you and all your household, for I have seen that you are righteous before me in this generation. Take with you seven pairs of all clean animals, the male and his mate, and a pair of the animals that are not clean, the male and his mate, and seven pairs of the birds of the heavens also, male and female, to keep their offspring alive on the face of all the earth. For in seven days I will send rain on the earth forty days and forty nights, and every living thing that I have made I will blot out from the face of the ground." And Noah did all that the Lord had commanded him.

Noah was six hundred years old when the flood of waters came upon the earth. And Noah and his sons and his wife and his sons' wives with him went into the ark to escape the waters of the flood. Of clean animals, and of animals that are not clean, and of birds, and of everything that creeps on the ground, two and two, male and female, went into the ark with Noah, as God had commanded Noah. And after seven days the waters of the flood came upon the earth (Genesis 7:1-10 ESV).

3. Joseph

"When Pharaoh was angry with his servants and put me and the chief baker in custody in the house of the captain of the guard, we dreamed on the same night, he and I, each having a dream with its own interpretation. A young Hebrew was there with us, a servant of the captain of the guard. When we told him, he interpreted our dreams to us, giving an interpretation to each man according to his dream. And as he interpreted to us, so it came about. I was restored to my office, and the baker was hanged."

Then Pharaoh sent and called Joseph, and they quickly brought him out of the pit. And when he had shaved himself and changed his clothes, he came in before Pharaoh. And Pharaoh said to Joseph, "I have had a dream, and there is no one who can interpret it. I have heard it said of you that when you hear a dream you can interpret it." Joseph answered Pharaoh, "It is not in me; God will give Pharaoh a favorable answer." Then Pharaoh said to Joseph, "Behold, in my dream I was standing on the banks of the Nile. Seven cows, plump and attractive, came up out of the Nile and fed in the reed grass. Seven other cows came up after them, poor and very ugly and thin, such as I had never seen in all the land of Egypt. And the thin, ugly cows ate up the first seven plump cows, but when they had eaten them no one would have known that they had eaten them, for they were still as ugly as at the beginning. Then I awoke. I also saw in my dream seven ears growing on one stalk, full and good. Seven ears, withered, thin, and blighted by the east wind, sprouted after them, and the thin ears swallowed up the seven good ears. And I told it to the magicians, but there was no one who could explain it to me."

Then Joseph said to Pharaoh, "The dreams of Pharaoh are one; God has revealed to Pharaoh what he is about to do. The seven good cows are seven years, and the seven good ears are seven years; the dreams are one. The seven lean and ugly cows that came up after them are seven years, and the seven empty ears blighted by the east wind are also seven years of famine. It is as I told Pharaoh; God has shown to Pharaoh what he is about to do. There will come seven years of great plenty throughout all the land of Egypt, but after them there will arise seven years of famine, and all the plenty will be forgotten in the land of Egypt. The famine will consume the land, and the plenty will be unknown in the land by reason of the famine that will follow, for it will be very severe. And the doubling of Pharaoh's dream means that the thing is fixed by God, and God will shortly bring it about. Now therefore let Pharaoh select a discerning and wise man, and set him over the land of Egypt. Let Pharaoh proceed to appoint overseers over the land and take one-fifth of the produce of the land of Egypt during the seven plentiful years. And let them gather all the food of these good years that are coming and store up grain under the authority of Pharaoh for food in the

> *cities, and let them keep it. That food shall be a reserve for the land against the seven years of famine that are to occur in the land of Egypt, so that the land may not perish through the famine"* (Genesis 41:10-36 ESV).

> *But now, do not therefore be grieved or angry with yourselves because you sold me here; for God sent me before you to preserve life. For these two years the famine has been in the land, and there are still five years in which there will be neither plowing nor harvesting. And God sent me before you to preserve a posterity for you in the earth, and to save your lives by a great deliverance. So now it was not you who sent me here, but God; and He has made me a father to Pharaoh, and lord of all his house, and a ruler throughout all the land of Egypt* (Genesis 45:5-8 NKJV).

I look at the lives of these three amazing men of God and what do I see?

1. I see three men who knew God.

2. I see three men who received divine strategy from God.
3. I see three men who obeyed God.

What do I see about the Lord in these verses?

1. I see He is the God who loves people.
2. I see He is the God who always has a redemptive strategy.
3. I see the God who always wants to rescue people.

So looking at the snippets of these stories included here, I want to encourage you with something. In this new era that we have entered, unlike any other time on earth we must be people who know the Lord, who seek to know His ways (Isaiah 55:11), who *seek* the divine strategy of God above all else, and people who *obey* the strategy of God.

It strikes me, too, how specific the Lord is in His strategy: Elijah sends the servant up seven times; Noah builds a boat with specific dimensions; and Joseph interprets Pharaoh's dream and receives the wisdom from God to prepare and position with supernatural revelation of divine strategy to preserve the life and bring great deliverance.

As I read passages like these, I am undone by the love of a good God and I am undone by the privilege that is given to the people of God to partner with Him in receiving revelation and divine strategy from the King of kings, the One who created the heavens and the earth, the Great I AM. This is not a privilege to be ever taken lightly; and I believe that right now what we are facing on earth and what we are moving into in this new era, God is calling for His people to have eyes to see and ears to hear, to move on the strategy of God in complete obedience to bring forth the redemptive strategy of the Lord and to see His Kingdom extended.

In the coming days of this new era, there will be greater warnings that the Lord will bring forth to those who are listening to the Lord and have their ears to His chest.

Hebrews 11:7 (NKJV) has been resounding loudly in my spirit for the last year—and for where we are right now on earth, it is resounding louder than ever:

> ***By faith Noah,*** *being divinely warned of things not yet seen, moved with godly fear, prepared an ark for the saving of his household, by which he condemned the world and became an heir of righteousness which is according to faith.*

God is going to release warnings of things to come in greater dimension in this new era. It is a call for the people of God to seek *His* strategy in the midst of it all, to release the Word of the Lord, to partner with the ways of God, and to see the strategy of the King implemented on earth to see His government established and His goodness and love revealed around the world.

When I was meditating on Hebrews 11:7, I couldn't get past these three words: *"By faith Noah."*

You know how I see *Noah's faith* demonstrated? He obeyed God! He moved on a word from the Lord and began to build a boat before the flood came. He heard a word from the Lord and He acted.

Elijah heard a word from the Lord that rain is coming. Before rain came, he went up on a mountain and positioned himself in intercession to cry out for the fulfillment of the Lord's word on earth.

Joseph received an invitation to interpret Pharaoh's dream, partnered with the Lord in delivering the interpretation, received favor and promotion, and then implemented the strategy of God.

All three of these characters were invited by God into His strategy; they responded and took their position in their obedience to the revelation of heavenly strategy to see the purposes of God extended on earth.

The New Normal Era

This is the era of the new normal. The era of the unexpected. The era when the people of God are to be living on the offense, not the defense. There are many things the Lord is doing through this shaking right now. He is raising up the true *Ecclesia* and He is positioning His people who hear and respond to begin to awake like never before and be positioned in offense rather than defense.

What does that look like?

It looks like a people arising knowing who their God is, living close to His heart, discerning His ways, living surrendered and *not* afraid to walk in the strategy of God no matter what it looks like.

My dear friend Larry Sparks said to me recently that he heard the Lord say, "Allow crisis to push you out of the box. Seek Me for the supernatural strategy and innovation that, in ordinary circumstances, you would not pursue Me for."

I hear the Lord resounding on this word. There is a significant invitation right now from the Lord to partner with Him in the *new* strategies that He is releasing. I want you to remember this—***new strategies!***

Things will not remain the same coming out of this coronavirus pandemic. The Church is going to see drastic changes as the Spirit of God moves once we regroup. There is going to be significant demonstrations of the hand of the Lord rearranging, changing, and the power of God coming in such significant ways that it is going to continue to shake what can be shaken and it will establish what God is establishing. The Lord is setting the stage—and He is realigning in the Church. We have to be people who more than ever are living on our faces crying out for the God's strategy.

The greatest mistake that could be made in this moment is to move forward in assumption that things are going to remain the same and miss the divine invitation of the Lord into the new strategies and divine innovation that He is releasing. He's releasing new strategies and new ways of doing things, and the fire of His purging upon the Church and the way we do Church right now positions us in the new wineskin to *receive* the new wine. But in order to carry the new wine, we must be ready to let go of what He says to let go of and embrace what He is releasing.

Part of the invitation into the new strategies the Lord is releasing is the unveiling and uncovering of things that stand in the way of the new strategies being implemented.

Some of the strategies and ways things were done before are about to be put to death to make room for the new blueprint and strategies of the Lord for the new era.

In the "putting to death" that will take place, the Lord showed me that in a local church context, He will reveal any areas where ministry has become an idol. He is shaking it and will bring it down to re-establish the Church in the place of awe of who He is and ministering to Him first as mentioned in Chapter 1. The fear of God that will come into the Church will solidify this in a greater way.

God spoke to me recently that He is weighing hearts right now and revealing areas of self-promotion. He is revealing areas of pride. This is where the Lord is bringing an intense shaking out of His love to position us. Think about it, Elijah, Noah, and Joseph all received strategy from the Lord that could have been seen as "out of the box." Joseph interprets Pharaoh's dream of a famine that hadn't even come yet; he receives strategy to prepare and some people may have thought he was crazy. Noah hears God say "build a boat" before the flood comes. Elijah "hears rain is coming" when the land is in drought and positions himself on a mountain to contend for the Lord's answer to come to pass. All three of these positions to obey the Lord's strategy required humility. Each put God's strategy first and foremost and radical obedience to what He was saying and releasing.

That's the position. Humility!

This world is not going to be changed and impacted by a comfortable church. This world is not going to be changed and impacted by a sleeping church. This world is not going to be changed and impacted by a church that is too afraid to step out on the Word of the Lord and the strategies of Heaven because of the fear of people and/or fear of the enemy.

This is the hour when God is raising up the true *Ecclesia*. Those who are laying down their lives for one person only—Jesus Christ. People with one agenda—to see His name glorified and their greatest devotion is to Him and His ways. They are so in love with Him that giving their lives every day is a joy, a privilege, an honor. This world is not going to be changed by the Church who has become familiar with God. This world is going to be changed by the burning ones who are living in the fear of the Lord, not in the fear of humans or fear of the enemy.

The Church has feared humanity and feared the enemy for too long. Now in this shaking, the Lord is preparing the Church for the greatest unveiling of Jesus Christ and His majesty that will restore awe to the Church. It will cause the true *Ecclesia* to run to Him and embrace Him. Those who are living in half-heartedness and complacency will run in the opposite direction. Is this the Lord's heart for people to run *from* Him? Absolutely not!

It's His *love* that is drawing people, and He will continue to draw people. But the shaking has begun in the Church to *loose us* from what has held us. A Church that is complacent and quiet will *not* change the world. It is the Church with a voice! A Church with authority! A Church who knows their Creator, knows His heart, and moves in *His* divine strategy that will see the earth changed and the Kingdom come in astounding ways in this new era.

Vault of Divine Innovation

I had an encounter with the Lord a few months ago, and I saw Jesus standing in front of a vault. He said, "I am opening up the vault of divine innovation."

What is innovation? It's a new method, idea, product. I feel this call resounding upon the Church right now—*divine innovation!*

I cannot articulate how crucial it is right now and going forward in this new era to lay everything down before the Lord and *listen*. It's time to *lie down and listen!* The divine strategy of God released in this moment and into this new era is to bring reformation to the Church, revival to the world, and awakening to the people of God. God wants to release divine innovation to His people to not only navigate times of crisis from the position of victory, but also in navigating the new move of His Spirit upon us—and to reveal *Jesus* as the answer to a world that does not know Him and transform society and culture.

In times of crisis we are to be people who carry the strategy of God and His wisdom to shine the light of

Jesus throughout the earth and the Gospel to be proclaimed farther and louder than ever before.

The creativity of God's heart is going to explode on earth through the Church and through those seeking His heart and listening to His ways for these new strategies. The time is upon us when the positioning of the Josephs will take place.

The time is upon us when they will be called upon to release the wisdom of God to those in power on earth in greater measure than we have ever seen. The positioning is coming to come for the people of God in days that are turbulent. The days ahead aren't going to be smooth sailing, but they will be days when the Church will arise like never before—those who are living close to the heart of the Lord, knowing Him intimately, living in the deep revelation of who He is and can stand in the midst of a storm and command it to silence in the name of Jesus Christ. The true *Ecclesia* is arising and will continue to arise in this hour. They do not take comfort in their own name or strength but live in the burning revelation of who He is and the power of His name.

Friend, there has been so much worship of humanity and of names in the Church that this mindset is being brought down. The fire of God is bringing that type of worship to the ground; and the One name that is going to be lifted high and worshiped in this new era louder than we have ever seen or heard is the name of ***Jesus.*** The worship of the name of Jesus first and foremost in the Church like we have never seen.

Encounter after encounter after encounter I have had with the Lord in the past six-twelve months have been about the idolizing of humankind—and that being removed in the Church. Jesus is taking His rightful place again. We are going to see the name of Jesus lifted high and glorified like never before in the Church, and then in the world! God wants to bring in the harvest, but He wants the Church ready to be able to carry the harvest that is going to come in. This shaking is happening, and accelerated preparation is happening to position the Church to be able to bring in the harvest.

This is the hour of Josephs! This is the hour of Esthers! As we pray for our leaders (1 Timothy 2:2) in this hour to have wisdom and to come to know the

Lord, there are going to be greater shakings and many of the world leaders will find themselves at their end—at the end of their wisdom in ways they have never experienced before—and they will turn to the Church in unprecedented levels seeking the wisdom of God. A frustration will come upon them in their own wisdom and they will begin to turn to the Josephs and the Esthers.

Have we begun to see that? Yes we have; but I believe we have only seen it as a small drop in the ocean compared to the scale it is going to take place on earth in this new era.

But for that to take place, we as *the Church must be ready*. We must be positioned; and part of that positioning is living continually close to His heart and seeking *His* strategies above all else, no matter the cost. This will be the era of the unexpected. The era when the Church is being called to live out of the boat.

It's time for the Church to walk on the water of His Word and out of the revelation of who Jesus is.

The shaking right now will reveal the dross so that we can take it to the Lord and allow Him to heal us. The shaking right now is revealing old strategies that need to be left and new strategies that need to be embraced.

The fire right now is revealing.

The fire is purifying.

The fire is testing.

The fire is refining.

You just watch in this new era how God will further demonstrate 1 Corinthians 1:27 (NLT):

> *Instead, God chose things the world considers foolish in order to shame those who think they are wise. And he chose things that are powerless to shame those who are powerful.*

Watch some of the astounding ways that the Gospel, the power of the Cross, the power of the blood, and the wisdom of God is going to be demonstrated in this new era that is going to show humankind that wisdom and power alone comes from *God* and is found in *Jesus Christ!*

So the invitation to you and me is this: Will we embrace the fire and be people who seek the strategy of God above all else and be the ones who walk by faith, living in the fear of the Lord, receiving heavenly strategy, bowing not to fear others, but establishing His government upon the earth to bring His purposes to pass on earth, being light, hope, and voices in a dark world.

It takes those who are living awake and alive to who He is, His Word, receiving His fresh strategies, letting go of control, and walking in obedience who will see great favor and promotion come upon them in this hour in many different ways and realms to see His Kingdom established.

Jesus is the answer proclaimed in all the earth!

Chapter 3

The Ferocious Focus of Faith and a New Level of Normal

The call to "come up higher" is resounding in the body of Christ in this new era. What do I mean by that? It's the call to victorious living. The Lord has spoken to me over and over again that He isn't raising up chickens, He is raising up eagles.

I had a vision where I saw many in the body of Christ running around on the ground like chickens. When I saw this vision there was a very strong sense of "living on the ground" and the phrase kept coming to me that I would often hear as a child in the school playground "You're a chicken," speaking of someone who is in fear and too scared to do something. There was a move of the Spirit and invitation to partner with the Lord to walk in a bold faith that has not been walked in before. The transitioning from the chicken to the eagle. The place of victorious living by faith.

In this new era, the Holy Spirit is maturing the saints in the Word of God and the decree of the Word. The Lord is bringing us further into our seat. Ephesians 2:6 says:

> *For He has raised us from the dead along with Christ and seated us with him in the heavenly realms because we are united with Christ Jesus* (NLT).
>
> *He raised us up with Christ the exalted One, and we ascended with him into the glorious perfection and authority of the heavenly realm, for we are now co-seated as one with Christ!* (TPT)

He is bringing us as His people further into the victory that is ours in Christ. He is teaching us as believers in this new era what it means to live by faith. To walk by faith and not by sight.

> *For we live by faith, not by sight* (2 Corinthians 5:7 NIV).

> *For we live by believing and not by seeing* (NLT).

This invitation upon us right now in this new era is to decide to take our stand upon the Word of God like never before. This era of unprecedented displays of His power and miracles is going to come through a people who live, breathe, feast, and walk upon the Word of God and live from that place.

The Amplified Bible version of Hebrews 11:3 says:

> *By faith [that is, with an inherent trust and enduring confidence in the power, wisdom and goodness of God] we understand that the worlds* (universe, ages) *were framed and created [formed, put in order, and equipped for their intended purpose] by the word of God, so that what is seen was not made out of things which are visible.*

So by the power of the Word of God and by faith we root and anchor our expectancy.

In the middle of 2018, I had an encounter with the Lord where He was continually speaking to me about the increase of faith that was coming in this new era upon the body of Christ. The Lord showed me the pressures, the battles, and the fires many have faced and are facing. But in the midst of the pressure, the pressing, and the opposition, the Spirit of God is raising up the people of God to a new level of faith. That's when the Holy Spirit whispered these words to me: "Lana, I am now raising My people up to a new level of normal."

I had a vision where I saw many of God's people being pushed into a corner, battle weary and feeling the intensity of the pressure, when suddenly Jesus appeared in front of them. He placed His hand on their chest and in the middle of the pressing and pressure, with such a weariness and panic on many faces, He spoke so gently but full of authority, "Look at Me! Look at Me!"

It was an invitation to look at nothing else but Him. He then spoke again and these words penetrated every part of me, "It's time for the ferocious focus of faith."

The definition of ferocious is savagely fierce, violent. Synonyms are intense, strong, powerful, extreme.

In the natural, ferocious has negative connotations; but when the Lord spoke it, my spirit leapt. It was the invitation to aggressively, violently, and passionately come against every situation, every opposition, every giant with such violent conviction of faith that says, "MY GOD SAID IT. HE PROMISED IT. HIS WORD IS TRUE. I AM NOT MOVING FROM IT!"

Matthew 11:12 is such a powerful verse that I want to look at it here and will also touch on it in the next chapter:

> *From the moment John stepped onto the scene until now, the realm of heaven's kingdom is bursting forth, and passionate people have taken hold of its power* (TPT).
>
> *From the days of John the Baptist until now the kingdom of heaven suffers violent assault,*

> *and violent men seize it by force [as a precious prize]* (Amplified Bible).

The vision continued. As the hand of Jesus was placed upon the chest of His people, I knew there was a major increase and impartation of faith taking place. Eye to eye in intense focus, gazes locked together, He spoke, "IT IS NOW TIME TO ROAR."

Suddenly I saw this fire burn within God's people. A fire of conviction of the *truth* and *power* of His Word and a righteous anger at what the enemy has stolen. The roar that burst forth out of the mouths of God's people was the Word of God, and it came with a boldness and conviction of faith greater than they had carried before. God says:

> *So shall my word be that goes out from my mouth; it shall not return to me empty, but it shall accomplish that which I purpose, and shall succeed in the thing for which I sent it* (Isaiah 55:11 ESV).

> *Is not my word like fire, declares the Lord, and like a hammer that breaks the rock in pieces?* (Jeremiah 23:29 ESV).

In this vision I see Jesus turn to me and He says, "Lana, pay attention to the roar. Listen to the roar. Listen to the sound of doubt being removed." I leaned in and listened to the roar of the conviction of truth and power of the Word flowing from the mouths of God's people; something deep was taking place in their hearts. It was such a deep awakening to who He was, that Jesus *is* the Word (John 1:1) and areas of unbelief were being exposed in the heart.

I started hearing a *loud* sound, the sound of *repentance.* The sound of repentance was loudly bursting from within hearts and out of mouths. Repentance for aligning with doubt and allowing natural realities and disappointments to fester in their hearts. I talk more about this later in this chapter.

God was bringing deep healing, deliverance, and freedom in the repentance, and He was increasing faith so significantly and the revelation of who He is and the power of His Word that doubt was being removed and a people were arising *strong* and *fortified.*

We are going to see a mighty wave of the Holy Spirit crash into the Church in this new era that will bring forth a major move of repentance. In September 2019, I had an encounter with the Lord and He said to me, "Lana, a *wave of travail* is about to crash into the Church in this new era." The Lord showed me that this wave of travail is coming with the restoration of the fear of the Lord to the Church. There is it again, *the fear of the Lord!*

I heard the Lord say, "My people are going to weep over sin again that will usher in the greatest move of holiness that has ever been seen." When the Lord spoke this, the sense surrounded me so strongly that this "weeping over sin" was not a place of condemnation nor was it a place of not living in the revelation of our identity in Christ and our righteousness before Him (2 Corinthians 5:21; Romans 3:22). Rather, it was the place of birthing no toleration of sin, the place of consecration, the place of purity being birthed in the

Church, because of our love, our awe and wonder of who He is as the King of kings and Lord of lords.

This deep repentance is going to take place in different ways in the Church in this new era to prepare us to carry the fire of His presence in ways we have never seen, and be able to carry the influx of the mighty harvest of souls that will come into the Kingdom along with mighty signs, wonders, and miracles.

Why am I sharing this with you? Because in this encounter the Lord exposed the areas of unbelief in the hearts of His people. Jesus refers to unbelief many times in Scripture and how it can hinder faith and the miraculous (Matthew 13:54-58, 17:20, 8:26). In this "new normal" of faith that God will raise the Church, He is going to expose unbelief in significant ways.

In one of the encounters I had with the Lord, I heard the Gospel being preached, but it shocked me when I saw *where* it was being preached—it was being preached *to the Church!*

I have shared with you in previous chapters about how the Lord is going to awaken the Church, in greater ways than we have ever seen, to the *power* of the Gospel and the finished work of the Cross and the power of His resurrection that will deal mightily with unbelief in hearts and the revelation of Jesus and His love at Calvary pouring into hearts in this new era. This increasing awakening is going to bring forth a greater level of repentance for areas of the heart full of unbelief and lead His people into a greater realm of victory that is already theirs in Christ (Romans 8:37). Kenneth Copeland says:

> Unbelief is believing something other than what God has said about a situation. You can believe Jesus was raised from the dead, you can believe He is your Lord, you can believe He is coming soon, but if you don't believe and do what He says, you are operating in unbelief. You can believe in Him, but still not believe what He says. The Bible calls this an evil heart—a hardened heart (Hebrews 3:12) and a heart of unbelief grieves God.[1]

The Lord is going to expose those areas of unbelief in the heart. Why? So we can move into a new level of normal and walk in the miraculous.

No Toleration

In this encounter with the Lord as the Spirit of God was dealing with unbelief and God's people were partnering with the conviction of His Spirit, I saw the intolerance within them increase. That intolerance for things in the natural that don't align with what God says, His purposes, plans and Kingdom. As the intolerance rose and faith rose, the giants standing in opposition to the Word of God began losing their hold as the people of God were arising with a fire in their belly that said, "NO MORE! I do not have to accept that for my life, my family, my city, my nation, the world. NOT ON MY WATCH!"

There was a greater awakening taking place regarding the standard and the normal—and that standard and normal was *The Word.* Where God's people had become chickens running on the ground and lowered their expectations and theology to meet their experience, God was now calling them higher ground, to stand on the Word of God alone and what He speaks (Matthew 4:4).

I remember the day a few years ago when God challenged me personally about this. One of my sons was sick and I messaged a friend and asked her to pray for him. She replied lovingly, "Of course I will pray for him, but remember Lana, it is normal for kids to get sick." As soon as I read that message, something didn't feel right in my spirit. I then heard the whisper of the Holy Spirit, "By whose definition of normal?"

In that moment I had an awakening. I realized that it's so easy to lower my expectation and my faith to "Of course kids get sick when they go to day care because it's a germ fest and it builds their immune system." While that's what the world says, is that the reality I'm going to live by? The Holy Spirit began to convict and challenge me—what normal am I going to live by? What the world says or even science or medicine says? Or am I going to live by the higher reality that has been purchased for me by Jesus?

I am grafted into Him, so I have access to all the promises of Scripture, including Psalm 91:10 (NET): *"No harm will overtake you; no illness will come near your home."* Is that just a nice saying that I can buy on a magnet and put on my fridge? Or is that the Word of God? A fire of conviction began to burn within me. I'm going to do what Bob Jones always said to do with God's Word, "Take it to the bank." By my faith I'm going to take what is promised to me and my family.

So in one moment, God had awakened me to a new level of normal in little things and areas I didn't even realize that I had allowed my faith and expectations to align with what was contrary to the Word of God.

Okay, back to the encounter...As this mighty move of the Spirit and awakening to faith and power of the Word of God (Hebrews 4:12) was taking place, I saw greater miracles, signs, wonders, and mighty demonstrations of His power taking place on the earth in intensity and acceleration.

I heard Him speak again, "Now is the time for greater access to what I have written in My books in the library of Heaven over individuals, cities, and nations as the faith of My people is increasing. While the chains of doubt remain, insight and clarity of what I am speaking was hindered. But now in this new era, as this increase and arising to a new level of normal is taking place, I am raising up an army, My army, branded with the fire of the conviction of Matthew 19:26, *'With God ALL things are possible.'*"

Looking straight into their eyes, Jesus replied, "Humanly speaking, no one, because no one can save themselves. But what seems impossible to you is never impossible for God." (See Matthew 19:26 TPT.)

This new era is being branded with Matthew 19:26. The impossible looking completely possible in Jesus. Think about salvation. *"While we were yet sinners, Christ died for us"* (Romans 5:8 ESV). He made a way where there was no way, now we walk in Him and by Him and in His authority to see the impossible become possible, not because of our human strength, but because of His power. This is the era when we will see the greatest demonstrations of impossibilities bow to the name of Jesus on a scale we have never seen.

The glorious awakening to the power in the name of Jesus will sweep the earth far and wide declaring the truth that He is Lord and one day every knee will bow and tongue confess that He is God (Philippians 2:10-11).

You may have walked many seasons of your life, especially in the last decade, that have been the most difficult. There have been so many battles, assaults, dark nights, and blazing fires; but through it all, He has been with you, holding you, encouraging you, loving you, strengthening you, and He has been doing a work deep within you that you may not even realize. Now in this new era, He is moving you out of the realm of disappointment and into the place of breakthrough, empowerment, strength, and maturity.

God is looking for those who will partner with His Spirit and be people of the Word that not only *know* the Word but *live* the Word and walk *on* the Word in obedience to it, by faith. This new era is going to see the people of God take bold steps of faith and see the mountains moved. We cannot partner with the Lord in all He is going to do in this new era if we are living from the ground as chickens, living by the natural realm, tossed to and fro and living in fear. Those who embrace the move of His Spirit, His maturing and are living in the Word by faith who will like eagles soar in the high places, living in victory.

Can I encourage you to take some time and ask the Holy Spirit if there are any areas of your life where you have being tolerating things, living lower than all that is yours in Christ? Like me, God used a text message to awaken to me a new level of normal to "not expect that kids just get sick" but pull me into the higher realm of the promise of Psalm 91:10. Ask the Holy Spirit if there are any areas in your heart and life that need attention. If He reveals any, repent for lowering your faith, ask for His truth, and let the Holy Spirit minister to your heart and encourage you in your faith.

You Will Not Fly

I heard the Lord speaking over the body of Christ recently, "While you live in the whys, you will not fly."

I was suddenly taken into a vision. I saw Jesus standing before the people of God and He was inviting them into new directions in this new era, new pathways, new adventures, new levels of exploration and faith, and He had His hand outstretched.

As the invitation was before them, I heard many people saying things like, "BUT WHY did this happen, Lord? BUT WHY did that happen?"

I then looked at their eyes and they were wearing sunglasses, and on their sunglasses was written the word "DISAPPOINTMENT." Everything that they were looking at was being viewed through the lenses of disappointment. What struck me strongly in that vision was that sunglasses can be removed. It is a choice to wear them. It was a choice to stay disappointed. This really struck me because it reminded me of the deep pain that I have felt in many seasons past when disappointment almost suffocated the life out of me. As I pondered this thought while watching the vision take place, I heard 1 Samuel 30:6 (ESV):

> *And* ***David was greatly distressed,*** *for the people spoke of stoning him, because all the people were bitter in soul, each for his sons and daughters. But David strengthened himself in the Lord his God.*

As I heard that Scripture loudly in this vision, I was surrounded by this strong thought. It doesn't say, "David was slightly upset," it says, *"David was greatly distressed."* Why? He had lost his two wives and people spoke of stoning him. Why? Because *"the people were bitter in soul."*

So I stopped and pondered for a while. David in that moment had every right to have a meltdown. David had every right in the natural to be in fear, to be incredibly discouraged and it says he was greatly distressed. But did he stop there? No! He chose in that moment to *strengthen himself in the Lord.* David rose above what was going on in his soul.

The Lord spoke to me in this vision; as I looked into the eyes of Jesus, I saw compassion, deep compassion for the pain and for the weariness that many have faced, but in His eyes I also saw a longing. It was a longing for His people to take His hand and through their faith, through their free will, through their ability to choose to not live in disappointment anymore and to take His hand and choose to believe again.

I remember thinking in this vision "Lord, disappointment is so heavy and it's hard to come out of it sometimes. Only your Spirit brings healing of disappointment." I heard the Lord say, "Look away from the disappointment. Lay down the whys, lay down the buts, and take off the sunglasses that are blocking the view of the Son."

It's a decision of the heart that says, "I am not going to live there anymore. I am not going to hold on to this anymore. I am going to center myself on Jesus."

I understood what the Lord was saying then. It was about focus. It was the place of realizing what I was actually focusing on. What am I rehearsing in my mind? If I am rehearsing the whys and the buts, then I'm not going to run in this new era—I'm going to remain stuck.

What did it look like for David to encourage himself in the Lord? The biblestudytools.com website says David:

> Took all patiently, and exercised his faith on his God; he encouraged himself in

> the power and providence of God; in the promises of God, and his faithfulness in keeping them; in view of his covenant relation to God, in remembrance of the grace, mercy, and goodness of God, and his former experiences of it; hoping and believing that God would appear for him in some way or another, and work salvation for him. The Targum is, "he strengthened himself in the Word of the Lord his God;" in Christ the Word of God, and in the power of His mighty, and in the grace that is in him (Ephesians 6:10, 2 Timothy 2:1)

David looked past the natural circumstances and looked to God. This is the call of maturity that the Lord is placing upon the body of Christ now as we move farther into this new era. We cannot be people who are led by our soul.

In this vision I *knew* that the healing, the grace, the anointing, and the freedom was coming in the place of the "letting go." There was a double-mindedness in the heart that was saying to Jesus, "I cannot come with You into the new. I cannot take Your hand again. I can't trust You again, because I don't understand why "x, y, z" happened to me." Jesus wasn't asking His people not to feel pain, He wasn't saying "Don't grieve" or "Get over it." There was a very strong sense in my vision of "unless I get the answers to the *whys*, I'm not moving, I can't move."

There was an invitation in this encounter to remove alignment from disappointment, to take off the glasses and look at Him. To encourage themselves in the Lord and not doubt who He is. To remind themselves of who He is—He is faithful, He never lies, He never fails, He is always the same. He is always working for our good. He is always taking us from glory to glory. What the enemy means for harm; God turns for good.

The only way I can describe the atmosphere in this encounter was that the love of Jesus was so strong for His people to accept his invitation to choose in this new era to run by taking Him at His Word—rather than stay stuck in their soul. God is healing disappointment; and as we move into this new era, we are moving from *"Hope deferred makes the heart sick" into "a dream fulfilled is a tree of life"* (Proverbs 13:12 NLT).

Jason Hooper, my friend and Senior Pastor of Kingsway Church in Alabama, shared a revelation with me recently that God gave him that is completely where we are right now:

> 2020 will be a year of what we have seen and said we are about to taste and see. A decade of disappointment has come to an end and a decade of declaration with demonstration has begun. I feel like many in the body of Christ have been in a Proverbs 13:12 holding pattern where *"Hope deferred has made the heart sick,* ***but*** *a desire fulfilled is a tree of life"* and from New Year's eve 2019 to January first 2020, we crossed over the big BUT. We went from the deferment of hope right into desire fulfilled.

I want you to receive that word today, friend. You are no longer in the holding pattern of the first half of Proverbs13:12 where hope has been deferred, that decade of disappointment, *but* you have now moved into the decade of declaration with demonstration. God is awakening us to the power of our decree *by faith* and then seeing the mighty demonstrations of His power to fulfill His Word.

This encounter where I saw Jesus leading His people out of disappointment, bringing healing, and seeing them choose not to live there anymore opened up to them a whole new realm and world of possibility, expectancy, and faith. Hope was being restored.

God's desire is to move the Church from *defense* to *offense*. We have to be people who are walking in the offense, rather than defense. Living led by our soul causes us to always live on the defense. Living in the revelation of who He is and His Word, how He sees and what He speaks by faith causes us to live on the offense. You are not fighting *for* victory; you are fighting *from* it.

The Giant of Fear

Fear is the opposite of faith. Faith is trust; fear causes us to run and withdraw if we agree and align with it. God spoke something so profound to me regarding the giant of fear in this new era: "If you are in fear of th
new era, you won't slay the giant of fear."

When He spoke that, it made total sense to me. If we are living in the place of fear of this new era and what it entails, what it requires, what will happen, etc., and we choose to put our faith and agreement in that place of fear, then we will not slay the giant of fear that will come against us.

One of the giants that will need to be slayed in this new era is the giant of fear, because we are moving in unchartered territory. There will be fear of the unknown, fear of stepping out, fear of other people, fear of rejection, etc., and if we bow and align to those areas of fear that raise their ugly heads to stop us from taking the new territories, then we will not slay the giants that stand before our promised lands.

Fear is always something that believers will battle; but the Lord showed me that the enemy is going to come [illegible] in intensity in this new era, so we must [illegible] at's where we live in *bold* faith. That's [illegible] l ourselves who is for us (Romans 8:31), [illegible] greater is He who is within me (1 John [illegible] ot give us a spirit of fear but of power [illegible] ind mind (2 Timothy 1:7).

The increasing revelation of Jesus Christ and the power of the Word of God that will increase in believers embracing the work of the Holy Spirit in this great maturing taking place are going to *slay* the giants of fear in this new era.

They will be the Davids arising as men and women after God's own heart with the stones of revelation in their hands of who their God I,s and stand before the giants declaring the same declaration that David did in 1 Samuel 17:26 (ESV): *"For who is this uncircumcised Philistine, that he should defy the armies of the living God?"*

That roar of faith rooted in the revelation of the nature and love of God is going to come out of believers living as friends of God. In this new era it will be a louder roar than we have ever heard and will stand with fire and conviction, declaring over situations that are opposite to what God is speaking, "Who do you think you are attempting to defy the Word of God and what the Lord is speaking?"

We are a people who live in and from their seat. A people who govern from their seat. A people who see Him and see the Word of the Lord and what He is speaking and move on it by faith, unshakeable and unstoppable, knowing that He will accomplish what He has spoken (Isaiah 55:11) and will tolerate nothing less than what He has promised.

Giants and fear may come but these ones are so consumed by the revelation of Jesus and who He is and His authority that they see not the problem before them but they see *Jesus as the only answer.* The perspective shift to greater realms of faith is and will continue to take place. A bold people will arise like never before.

This is the place where we don't stand and live in the natural realm, but by every Word that flows from His mouth (Matthew 4:4). If we live there, we are unstoppable, not caged in fear. When we live in the place of relationship with Him where we hear what He is saying and feasting on the Word, filling our hearts with truth, *that* frames every part of our lives as we position ourselves in faith and expectation that God is not a liar.

God is faithful and will do what He says He will do. It may look different from how we expect or when we expect it to happen, but the way He moves is always greater than our expectation (Ephesians 3:20). God is raising up a people with fortified, strong, mature faith muscles—those who have been through the fire and remained. Those who have their roots in one Person only—Jesus Christ. The One who never changes. The One who is the same yesterday, today, and forever. The ferocious focus of faith.

It's not hard. It's simple. Keep your eyes in one place. Locked with His. Because when you see Jesus and look into His eyes and see that He is the answer, He is the Word, and you believe what you see, nothing will be impossible for you.

Endnote

1. "3 Ways to Overcome Unbelief," March 20, 2018, Kenneth Copeland Ministries; https://blog.kcm.org/3-ways-overcome-unbelief/; accessed March 29, 2020.

Chapter 4

Meditate on the Fresh Manna—You Are Being Fortified

I heard the Lord say these words, which are not just about the coronavirus pandemic—but a key for this new era: "Meditate on the Manna, not the media."

Right now when you turn on the television you will see the fear being proclaimed through the airwaves. The Lord showed me that the enemy is shouting fear and terror all around the earth right now. But there is an invitation upon the Church to draw close to Jesus, go deep with Him into the Garden, allow the alignment of His hand and love to take place in hearts and lives, and step into *new manna*.

The Lord is releasing new manna right now in unprecedented levels. The revelation that the Lord is releasing is deep, it's the secrets of His heart, the keys for this new era and navigating this incredible time we have arrived at as the Church. The time of reset, the time of reformation, the time of refining, the time of running with Him like never before.

I had a vision of people drawing close to Jesus in the Garden; and while in communion with Him, scales were falling off their eyes. I believe the Lord is giving His people eyes to see and ears to hear in this moment like never before, as they draw near to Him in surrender and yielding.

There may be a storm blowing around loudly over the earth, but the Lord is drawing His people into His heart where they find refuge (Psalm 91). The hand of God is centering the Church on Him! The Lord wants to remind His people in this hour that He is our Rock.

Psalm 18:2 says:

> *The Lord is my rock, my fortress, and my deliverer, my God, my rock, in whom I take refuge, my shield, and the horn of my salvation, my stronghold* (ESV).

> *You're as real to me as bedrock beneath my feet, like a castle on a cliff, my forever firm fortress, my mountain of hiding, my pathway of escape, my tower of rescue where none can reach me. My secret strength and shield around me, you are salvation's ray of brightness shining on the hill-side, always the champion of my cause* (TPT).

God is fortifying the Church and strengthening His people to stand in Him alone. He is asking: Where do you find your peace? Where do you find your joy? Where do you find your hope? There are so many questions the Lord is asking, and I see each question is a wrapped gift being sent to us. Why? Because those questions are invitations to draw closer to Him. If we find our answers are anything but Jesus, we can embrace His grace, His love, and His invitation—and in repentance draw close to Him. He is raising up the true Church who are strong and are not shaken by circumstances but standing in and upon the Rock.

My oldest son Elijah was coloring this morning and he came to show me his picture. At the bottom of his page was a quote by Robert H. Schuller: "Tough times never last, but tough people do." It spoke to me and brought me right back to what the Lord was saying. Tough times don't last forever, but the fortifying that takes place in those tough times is the strength built within people that causes them to remain. It's the gift of endurance, it's the gift of strength, it's the gift of perseverance. It's the gift of the birthing of the overcomer.

Right now the enemy has come hard against the world with this virus, but what the enemy intended, God has used to give a gift to the Church. Fortification! Don't be surprised if you look back at this time in 2020 and see that you yielded to Him, that some of the greatest encounters, deliverance, healing, freedom, impartation, and preparation took place in this moment. Because that's what He's like! He's that good.

Even in this moment when the Lord is correcting things (Hebrews 12:6), He is doing so in His glorious love to draw His people closer to Him and to position them in alignment to run with Him like never before. He's calling for focus, He's calling for the returning to the First Love (Revelation 2:4) because that's where you were created to live. That's the place of life. Your greatest purpose on this earth is to *know Him!* Then make Him *known!*

So here we are in this moment of *selah* in this moment where there is a glorious invitation upon us. God is pouring out significant revelation. We are being called into position and right alignment. I believe the Lord is calling us to *anchor in the Word* like never before. I talked a lot about *ferocious faith* in the chapter previously, but the Lord is really highlighting meditating on the Word.

There is a serious demonic attack of distraction that has come in this new era, and it will continue, but God is giving us the keys right now to fight off distraction. I believe God is calling us deeper into His Word.

> *Keep this Book of the Law always on your lips; meditate on it day and night, so that you may be careful to do everything written in it. Then you will be prosperous and successful* (Joshua 1:8 NIV).

> *May these words of my mouth and this meditation of my heart be pleasing in your sight, Lord, my Rock and my Redeemer* (Psalm 19:14 NIV).

God is really bringing to our attention what we focus on right now, what we meditate on. In accepting the invitation to meditate on God's Word, the Bible, day and night, God is releasing revelation that is needed for you, for me, for the Church to navigate this new era.

Some of the pathways God has for you in this new era that are changing right now are going to come to you through the *rhema* Word of God. The understanding for the time and season we are in will be found in His presence and meditating on the Word. Don't allow your mind to be filled with anything except what He is saying. This is an era to *occupy,* and God is leading His people into right alignment so we can occupy what He has spoken and promised and extend His Kingdom on earth.

Right now the enemy is attempting to occupy the minds and hearts of people through fear. So, the alignment of your heart and mind right now is *very* important (Romans 12:2). The enemy wants your eyes to see fear and all the things he is doing. But God is saying to look up higher! See all the great and mighty things He is doing on earth for His people. He will tell us remarkable secrets we do not know about yet (Jeremiah 33:3 NLT). There is such a major perspective shift taking place right now where the Lord is calling His people into the place of focus on what *He* is speaking (Matthew 4:4) and what *He* is doing.

My beautiful friend Katherine Ruonala has said in recent days that she feels the stirrings of personal revival taking place as well as the outpouring coming on earth. There is indeed a personal revival taking place right now in the Church and it is coming through the shaking. There is fire in the Garden.

For years God has been highlighting to me the story of Moses and the burning bush in Exodus 3, and I know Katherine Ruonala and others are speaking from this story recently too. The Lord is bringing this story to the forefront again.

A few years ago the Lord said to me, "Lana, look at the words in verse 4."

> *When the Lord saw Moses coming to take a closer look, God called to him from the middle of the bush, "Moses! Moses!" "Here I am!" Moses replied* (Exodus 3:4 NLT).

Moses came to take a closer look at something that was unexpected and out of ordinary in the sense that this bush didn't stop burning.

Here we are in a moment on earth that has taken the world by surprise. It's unexpected in some ways, and many people feel like their whole world has been shaken and turned upside down. But in this moment, do we take a closer look? Do we stop, *selah,* pause, and reflect instead of meditating on what the media is saying and what the world is saying. Do we look up to Him from where our help comes (Psalm 121) and say, "GOD, what are YOU seeing? What are YOU saying?"

Friend, this is where the bride of Christ—the Church—arises in authority. This is where the bride arises in unity. This is where the Bride arises on earth as the light. This is where the bride arises victorious. The shakings cause the Church to awake! My encouragement is to ask yourself, *What am I meditating on? Who am I listening to?*

This is such a glorious invitation to look into the eyes of Jesus right now. His eyes are like flames of fire as it says in Revelation 19:12, and His loving gaze is drawing you. In the fire in the Garden right now, His fiery eyes await you. In His eyes you will see peace; in His eyes you will see joy; in His eyes you will see strength; in His eyes you will see healing; in His eyes you will see freedom and deliverance. This is your hour of alignment, healing, deliverance, freedom, and consecration to Him (Joshua 3:5).

> ***Set your mind on things above,*** *not on things on the earth. For you died, and your life is hidden with Christ in God. When Christ who is our life appears, then you also will appear with Him in Glory* (Colossians 3:2-4 NKJV)*).*

It's time to truly *set your mind on things above.* This fortification taking place in this crisis is the Lord preparing and teaching His people how to walk by faith and not by sight; for the trials will continue to come, but do you walk in the trials and be knocked around by them or do you walk above them in peace and authority in Christ?

Take time to be in the Garden with Him and let Him reveal to you what is to come. Creativity is going to be birthed like we have never seen from the Garden place in this *selah* moment.

Commissioning

There is a commissioning taking place in the Garden right now. In the *selah* moment with Jesus, there is a great commissioning taking place. What the Spirit of God reveals to you in this time is going to commission you to go forth as a light on earth in unprecedented ways. Moses was commissioned from the burning bush. You are being commissioned into new things from this point in this new era as you align and yield.

There are new ventures, pathways, and assignments that God has for you. You are going to receive the impartation, anointing, vision, and strategy for this moment. So, God is drawing you to meditate on His Word, the revelation He is releasing for that is where your positioning, deliverance, healing, and commissioning is taking place. We must be people of the Word. This is where the maturing happens. This is where the fortifying happens.

Rest in the Reset

I leave you with these words that God whispered into my heart, "There is rest in the reset."

This global reset is taking place on earth and there seems to be no rest; yet God is saying that in the Garden, in the positioning of alignment and surrender, *there is rest in the reset.* He is bringing rest to His people. Faithful people rest (Hebrews 11); they rest in their First Love; they rest in healing; they rest in deliverance; and they rest that comes in refreshment.

Yes, as the earth is shaking and people are scared and anxious at the loss of control, God is bringing peace to

His fortified people as they meditate upon Him and His Word, so they can go forth and speak the love and peace of Jesus to a world that is in incredible fear. God is calling His people into a higher rest knowing who He is and His nature and His love. His love will so overwhelm you in the Garden as you draw near that it will cast out all fear (1 John 4:18).

He is training us to reign!

Let all the voices of the world and fear and anxiety fall away as you meet Him in the Garden and lie down (Psalm 23), trusting in your Good Shepherd, meditating on the fresh manna, and yielding to His fire of preparation.

For there you *will* find rest.

I'll see you in the Garden, where everything changes!

A Final Encouragement

During the last week or so, the story of Elijah and the prophets of Baal has strongly been on my heart. Let's look at the biblical account together:

Elijah's Message to Ahab

> *And it came to pass after many days that the word of the Lord came to Elijah, in the third year, saying, "Go, present yourself to Ahab, and I will send rain on the earth."*
>
> *[2]So Elijah went to present himself to Ahab; and there was a severe famine in Samaria. [3]And Ahab had called Obadiah, who was in charge of his house. (Now Obadiah feared the Lord greatly.*
>
> *[4]For so it was, while Jezebel massacred the prophets of the Lord, that Obadiah had taken one hundred prophets and hidden them, fifty to a cave, and had fed them with bread and*

water.) [5]And Ahab had said to Obadiah, "Go into the land to all the springs of water and to all the brooks; perhaps we may find grass to keep the horses and mules alive, so that we will not have to kill any livestock." [6]So they divided the land between them to explore it; Ahab went one way by himself, and Obadiah went another way by himself.

[7]Now as Obadiah was on his way, suddenly Elijah met him; and he recognized him, and fell on his face, and said, "Is that you, my lord Elijah?"

[8]And he answered him, "It is I. Go, tell your master, 'Elijah is here.'"

[9] So he said, "How have I sinned, that you are delivering your servant into the hand of Ahab, to kill me? [10]As the Lord your God lives, there is no nation or kingdom where my master has not sent someone to hunt for you; and when they said, 'He is not here,' he took an oath from the kingdom or nation that they could not find you. [11]And now you say, 'Go, tell your master,

"Elijah is here"'! [12]And it shall come to pass, as soon as I am gone from you, that the Spirit of the Lord will carry you to a place I do not know; so when I go and tell Ahab, and he cannot find you, he will kill me. But I your servant have feared the Lord from my youth. [13]Was it not reported to my lord what I did when Jezebel killed the prophets of the Lord, how I hid one hundred men of the Lord's prophets, fifty to a cave, and fed them with bread and water? [14]And now you say, 'Go, tell your master, "Elijah is here."' He will kill me!"

[15]Then Elijah said, "As the Lord of hosts lives, before whom I stand, I will surely present myself to him today."

[16]So Obadiah went to meet Ahab, and told him; and Ahab went to meet Elijah.

[17]Then it happened, when Ahab saw Elijah, that Ahab said to him, "Is that you, O troubler of Israel?"

[18]And he answered, "I have not troubled Israel, but you and your father's house have, in that you have forsaken the commandments of the Lord and have followed the Baals. [19]Now therefore, send and gather all Israel to me on Mount Carmel, the four hundred and fifty prophets of Baal, and the four hundred prophets of Asherah, who eat at Jezebel's table."

Elijah's Mount Carmel Victory

[20]So Ahab sent for all the children of Israel, and gathered the prophets together on Mount Carmel. [21]And Elijah came to all the people, and said, "How long will you falter between two opinions? If the Lord is God, follow Him; but if Baal, follow him." But the people answered him not a word. [22]Then Elijah said to the people, "I alone am left a prophet of the Lord; but Baal's prophets are four hundred and fifty men. [23]Therefore let them give us two bulls; and let them choose one bull for themselves, cut it in pieces, and lay it on the wood,

but put no fire under it; and I will prepare the other bull, and lay it on the wood, but put no fire under it. [24] *Then you call on the name of your gods, and I will call on the name of the Lord; and the God who answers by fire, He is God."*

So all the people answered and said, "It is well spoken."

[25]*Now Elijah said to the prophets of Baal, "Choose one bull for yourselves and prepare it first, for you are many; and call on the name of your god, but put no fire under it."*

[26]*So they took the bull which was given them, and they prepared it, and called on the name of Baal from morning even till noon, saying, "O Baal, hear us!" But there was no voice; no one answered. Then they leaped about the altar which they had made.*

[27]*And so it was, at noon, that Elijah mocked them and said, "Cry aloud, for he is a god; either he is meditating, or he is busy, or he is*

on a journey, or perhaps he is sleeping and must be awakened." [28]*So they cried aloud, and cut themselves, as was their custom, with knives and lances, until the blood gushed out on them.* [29]*And when midday was past, they prophesied until the time of the offering of the evening sacrifice. But there was no voice; no one answered, no one paid attention.*

[30]*Then Elijah said to all the people, "Come near to me." So all the people came near to him. And he repaired the altar of the Lord that was broken down.* [31]*And Elijah took twelve stones, according to the number of the tribes of the sons of Jacob, to whom the word of the Lord had come, saying, "Israel shall be your name."* [32]*Then with the stones he built an altar in the name of the Lord; and he made a trench around the altar large enough to hold two seahs of seed.* [33]*And he put the wood in order, cut the bull in pieces, and laid it on the wood, and said, "Fill four waterpots with water, and pour it on the burnt sacrifice and on the wood."* [34]*Then he said, "Do it a second time," and they did it a second*

time; and he said, "Do it a third time," and they did it a third time. [35]*So the water ran all around the altar; and he also filled the trench with water.*

[36]*And it came to pass, at the time of the offering of the evening sacrifice, that Elijah the prophet came near and said, "Lord God of Abraham, Isaac, and Israel, let it be known this day that You are God in Israel and I am Your servant, and that I have done all these things at Your word.* [37]*Hear me, O Lord, hear me, that this people may know that You are the Lord God, and that You have turned their hearts back to You again."*

[38]*Then the fire of the Lord fell and consumed the burnt sacrifice, and the wood and the stones and the dust, and it licked up the water that was in the trench.* [39]*Now when all the people saw it, they fell on their faces; and they said, "The Lord, He is God! The Lord, He is God!"*

> [40]*And Elijah said to them, "Seize the prophets of Baal! Do not let one of them escape!" So they seized them; and Elijah brought them down to the Brook Kishon and executed them there* (1 Kings 18:1-40 NKJV).

Do you know what the Lord told me to do with this passage here at the end of this book? He said, "Lana, let Scripture speak for itself."

So I leave this passage here for you to meditate on, for you to ask the Lord what He is saying to you right now through this story. I believe the Lord wants to reveal some revelations to you through this passage of Scripture from His Word. This is one of the Bible stories for the hour we are in.

So I ask you...

What do you see?

What do you hear?

Do you know what I hear? God is about to reveal Himself to the earth and to the Church as the One and Only true God who holds *all* power and authority! I hear the sound of the Church rising up worshipping Him in Spirit and in truth (John 4:24).

It's time for a great unveiling and a great returning!

> *And being found in appearance as man, He humbled Himself and became obedient to the point of death, even the death on the cross. Therefore God also has highly exalted Him and given Him the name which is above every name, that at the name of Jesus every knee should bow, of those in heaven, and those on earth, and of those under the earth, and that every tongue should confess that* ***Jesus Christ is Lord, to the glory of God the Father*** (Philippians 2:8-11 NKJV).

About the Author

Lana Vawser grew up in the Sutherland Shire, in New South Wales, Australia. She began her relationship with Christ in 1996, soon after which she started to understand and grow in her prophetic gifting both to individuals and the greater body of Christ. Since then she has ministered in various roles in local churches while posting prophetic messages through email lists or online. Lana has been featured regularly on *The Elijah List*, *The Australian Prophetic Council*, and occasionally in *Charisma* magazine.

Lana Vawser has a heart to encourage the body of Christ and individuals in their walks with Jesus, deeper intimacy with Him, and learning to hear His voice. Lana operates in the prophetic and loves to share the heart of God with others. Lana's first book, titled *Desperately Deep—Developing Deep Devotion and Dialogue with Jesus*, was followed by her second, *The Prophetic Voice of God.* She is a gifted prophet and teacher and loves to see others grow in all that God has for them.

Lana earned her Bachelor of Ministry degree from Tabor College, Sydney. She and her husband, Kevin, co-pastored a church; he is gifted prophetically and pastorally with discernment. Kevin joins Lana as a speaker and also manages the ministry.

Kevin and Lana have three young boys, Elijah, Judah, and Benjamin. They mostly journey and minister as a family, and hope to raise up other sons, daughters, mothers, and fathers to journey with Christ in ministry and wonder. They reside in Adelaide, South Australia.

Made in the USA
Coppell, TX
30 August 2021